Raphael's Orchard

DESIGNED BY: IVO
EDITED BY: AVIRAM TRACHTENBERG

Gather around and listen to a unique story,

today we will
learn how an
orchard grows
to glory.

Raphael
is a
very
humble
man.

He plants trees,
a quiet and calm orchard
farmer, working with the bees.

He loves to tend
to his orange
trees,
large trees with
green leaves.

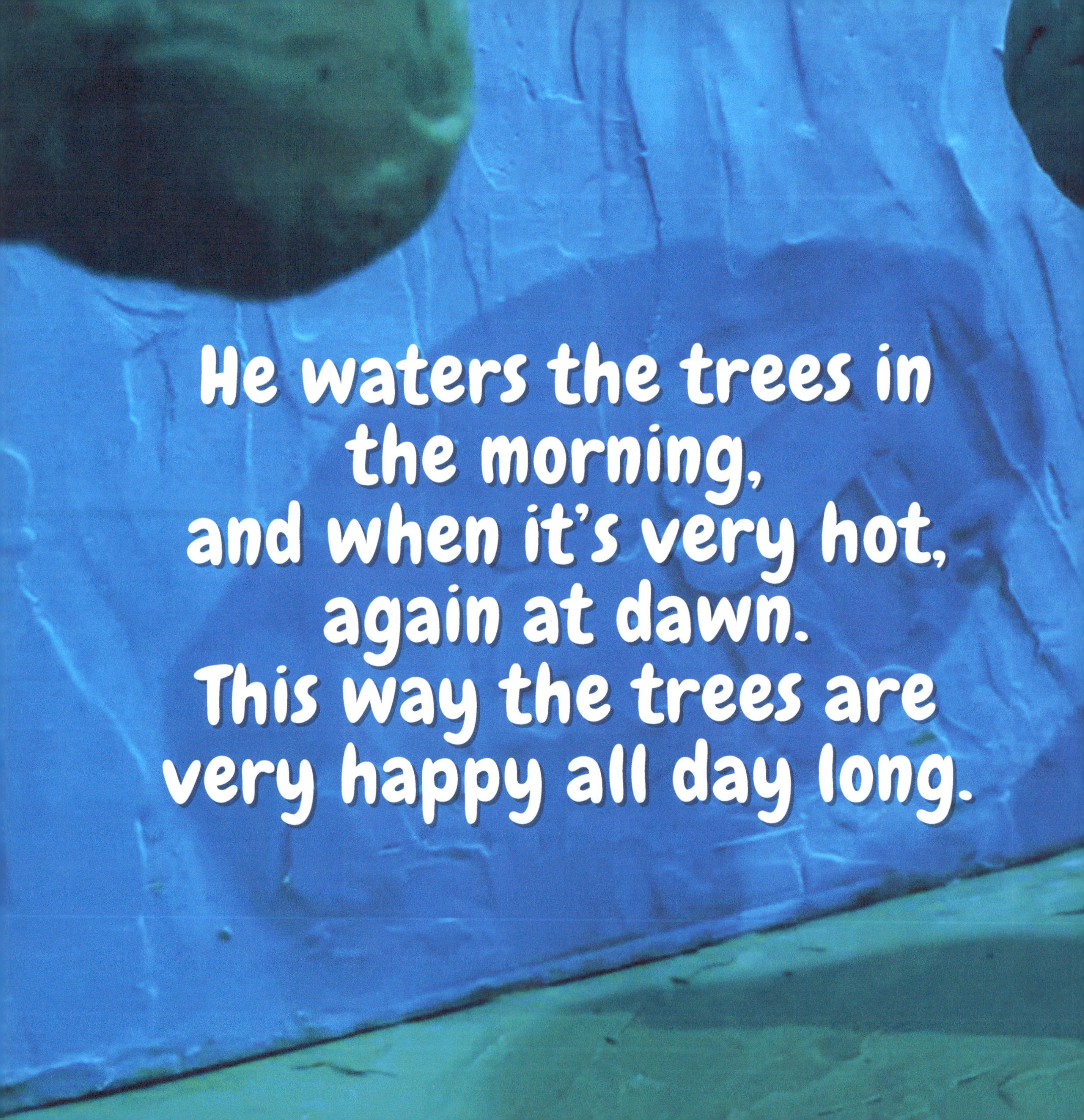
He waters the trees in
the morning,
and when it's very hot,
again at dawn.
This way the trees are
very happy all day long.

The trees grow bigger
every moment of each
day.

Soon ...
you will smell
the blossom scent

from far away.

He loves
to give them
lots of attention.

He dances,
sings
and
fills their
imagination.

In the beautiful orchard, a lot of oranges are picked by hand, and then, to a packaging factory, they are sent.

Later, they are distributed to all the fruit and vegetable stores,

welcoming
customers with
open doors.

One day in Raphael's orchard, stormy winds broke out in a rage,

they were
so strong
they broke
the water
gauge.

Leaves flew in
the air,
the branches
broke
with a very
loud sound

and all the
oranges fell to
the ground.

Raphael was very sad.
He stopped singing,
laughing and even
dancing, as things were
very bad.

The packaging factory
refused to receive any
fruit,
because they were so very
muddy and packed with
dirt.

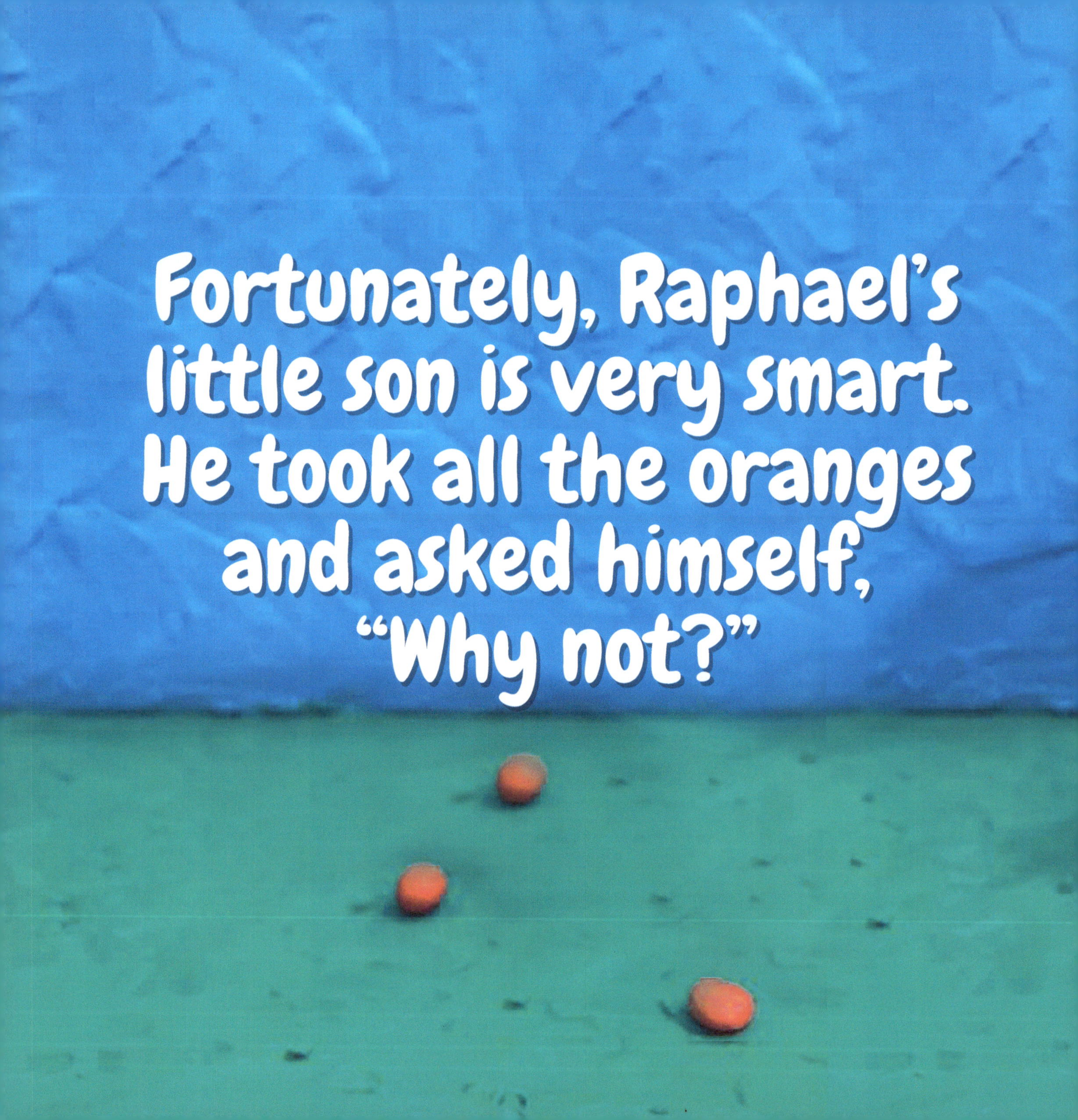

Fortunately, Raphael's little son is very smart. He took all the oranges and asked himself, "Why not?"

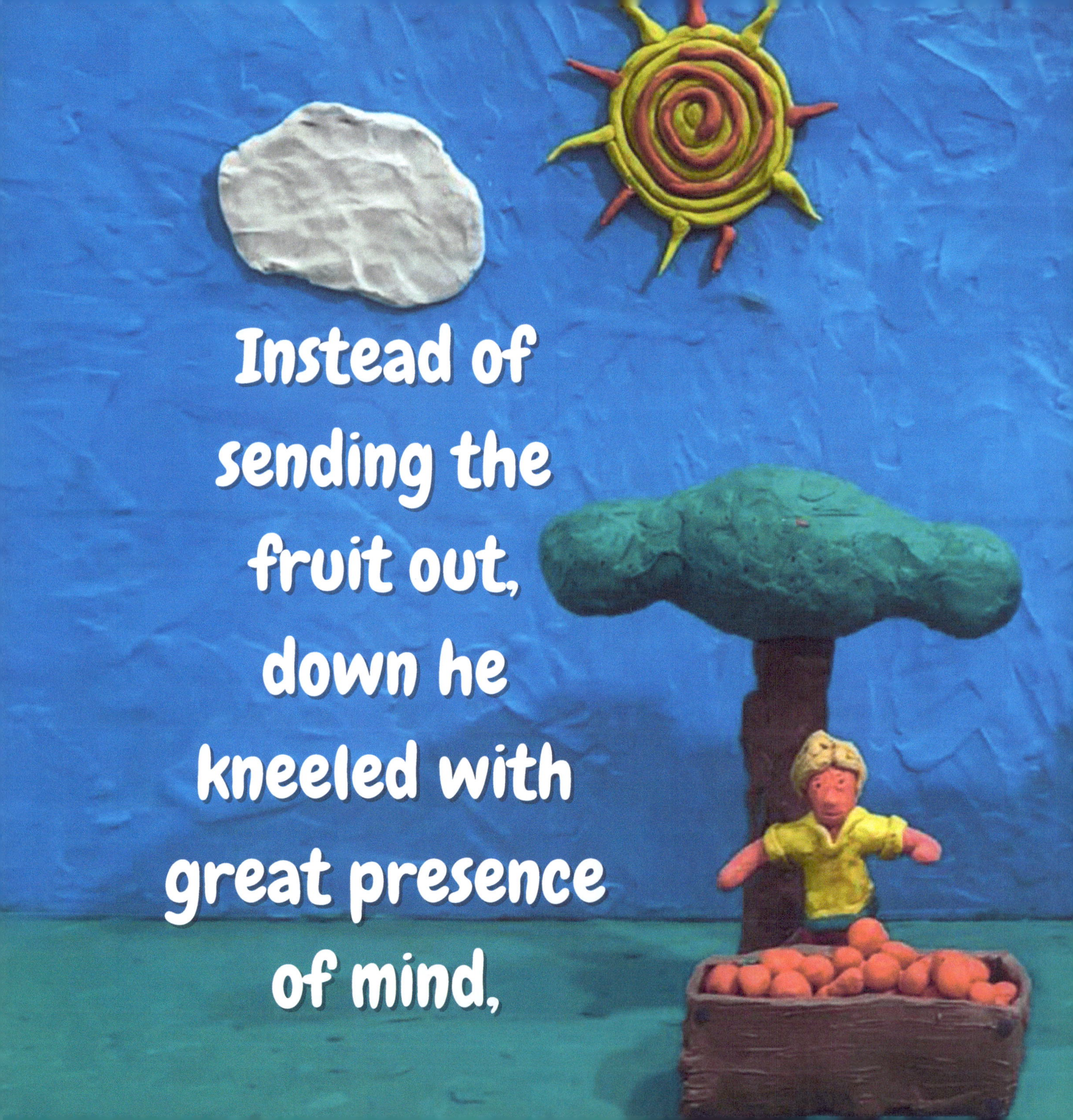

Instead of
sending the
fruit out,
down he
kneeled with
great presence
of mind,

to pick up from the
ground
every orange he could
find.

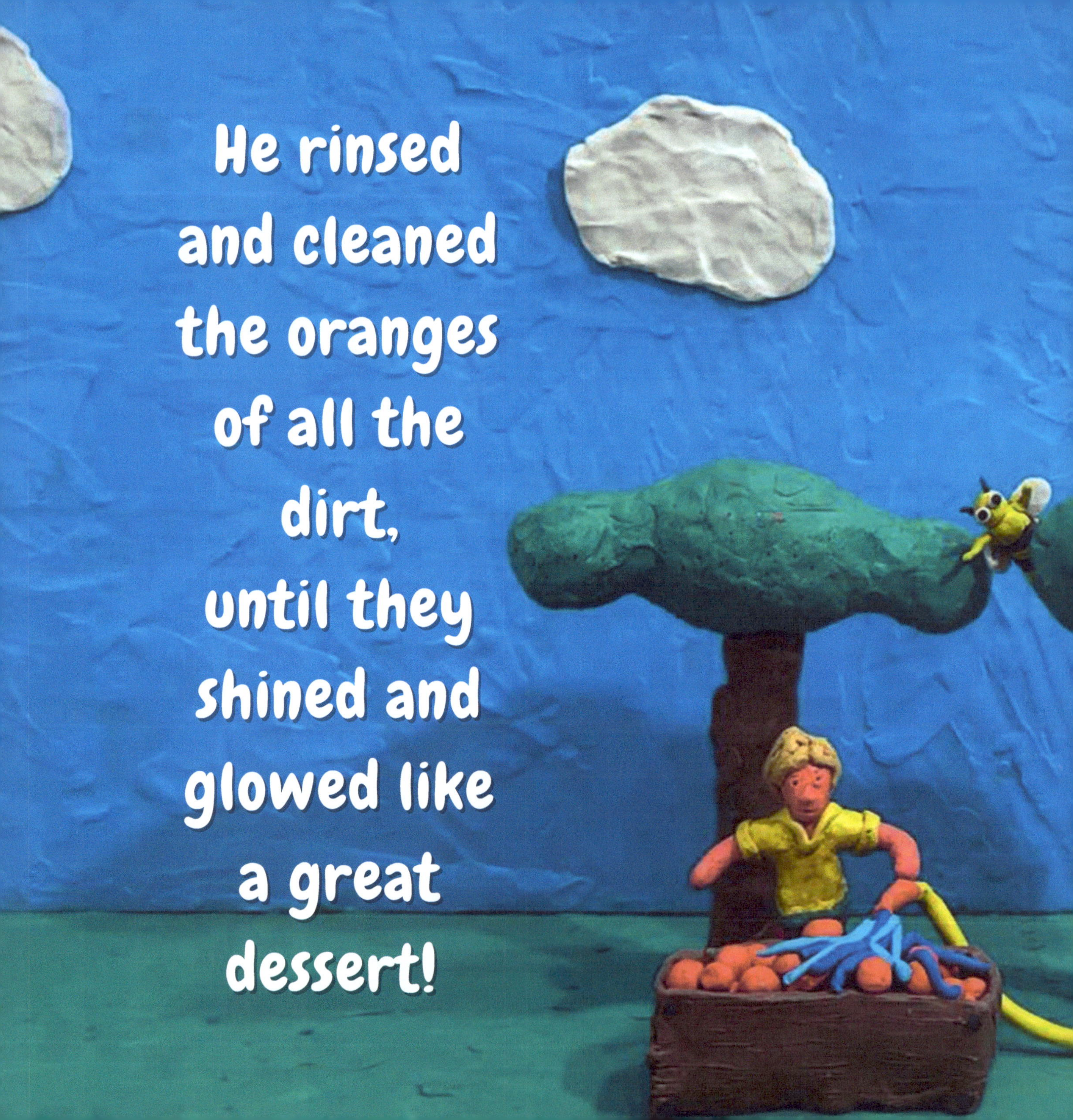

He rinsed
and cleaned
the oranges
of all the
dirt,
until they
shined and
glowed like
a great
dessert!

He shouted
out and
rang a bell,
"Great yummy
oranges for sale!"

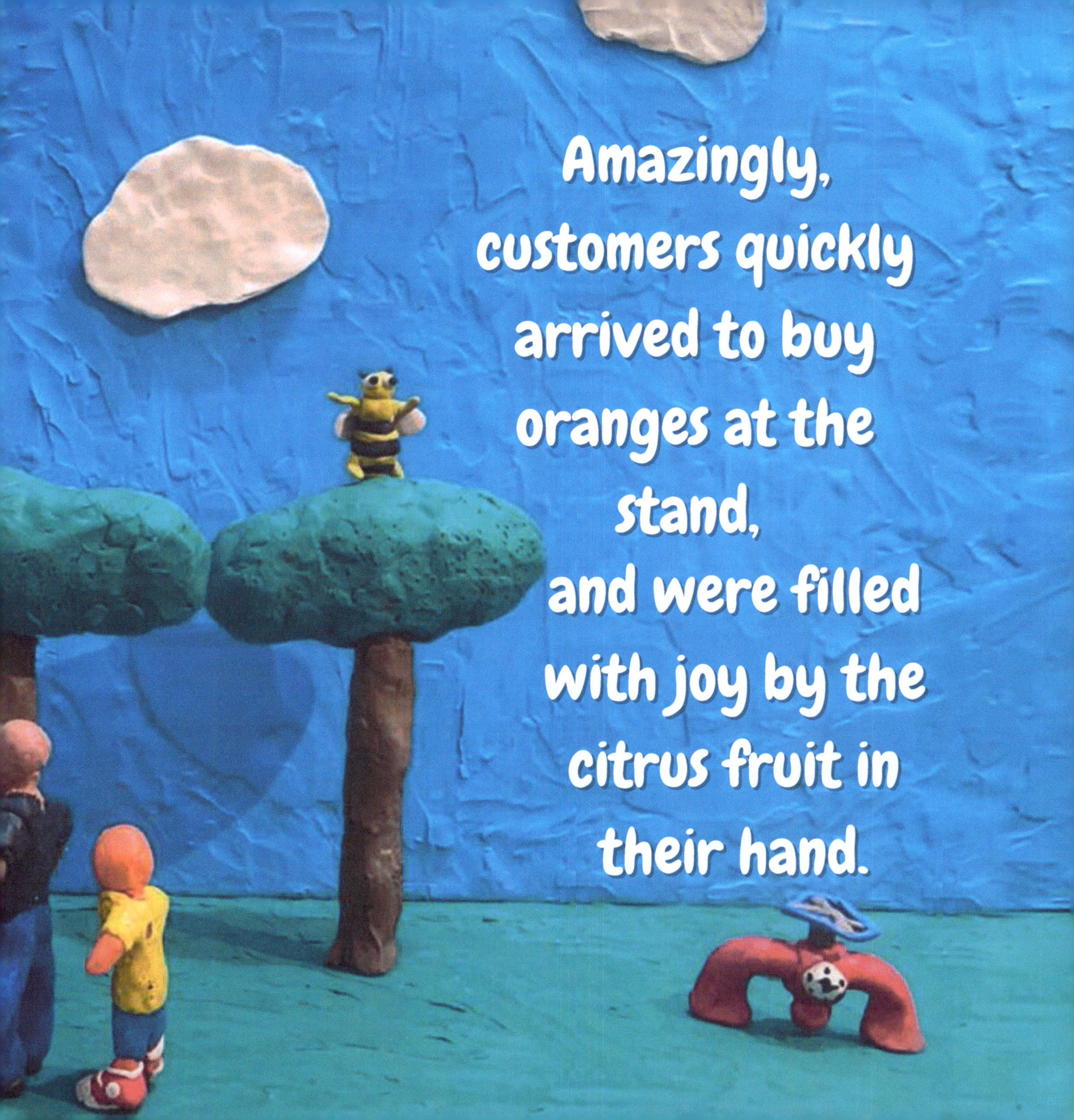

Amazingly,
customers quickly
arrived to buy
oranges at the
stand,
and were filled
with joy by the
citrus fruit in
their hand.

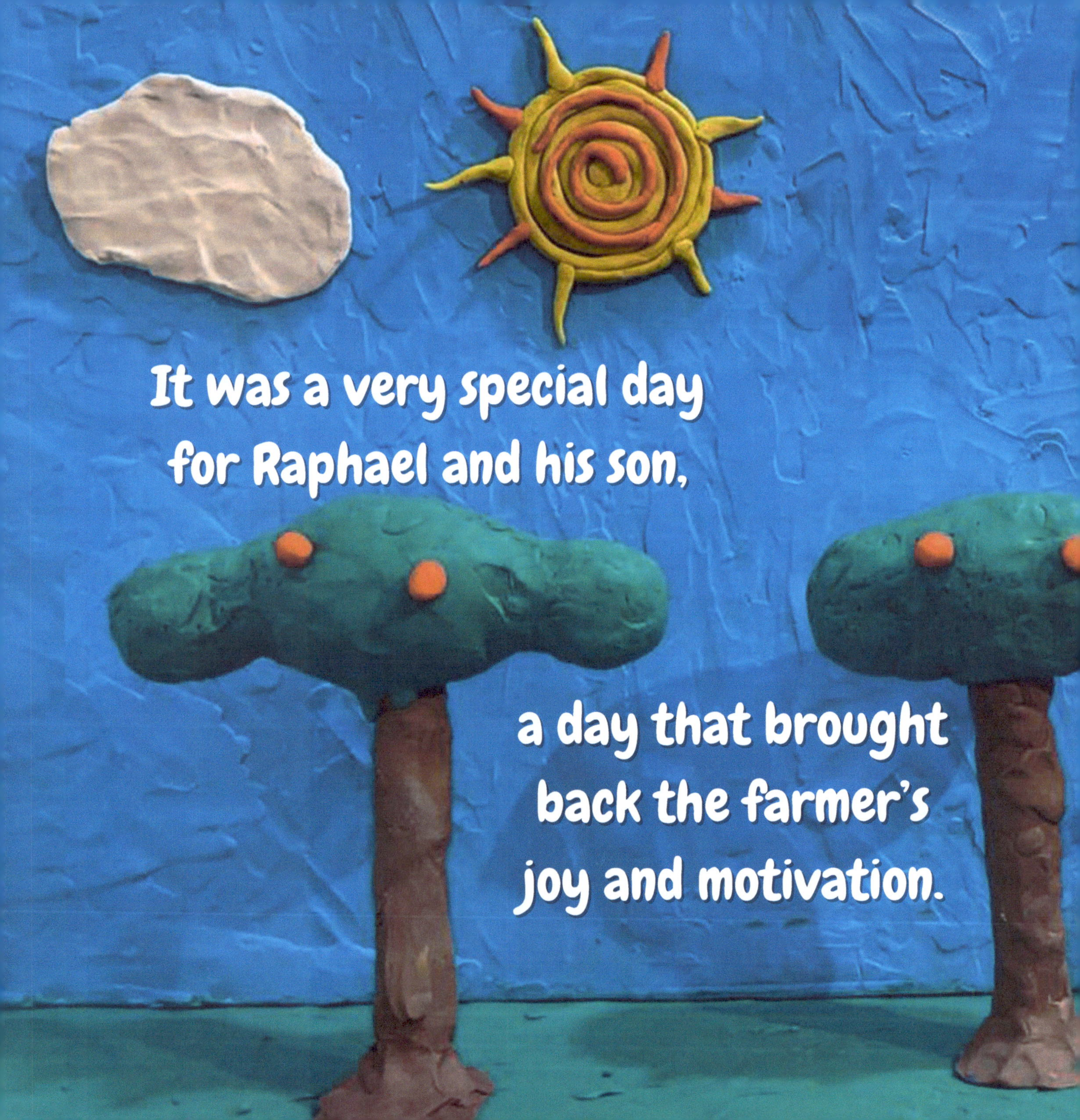
It was a very special day
for Raphael and his son,

a day that brought
back the farmer's
joy and motivation.

Once again, he sang, laughed and danced with the trees of his creation.

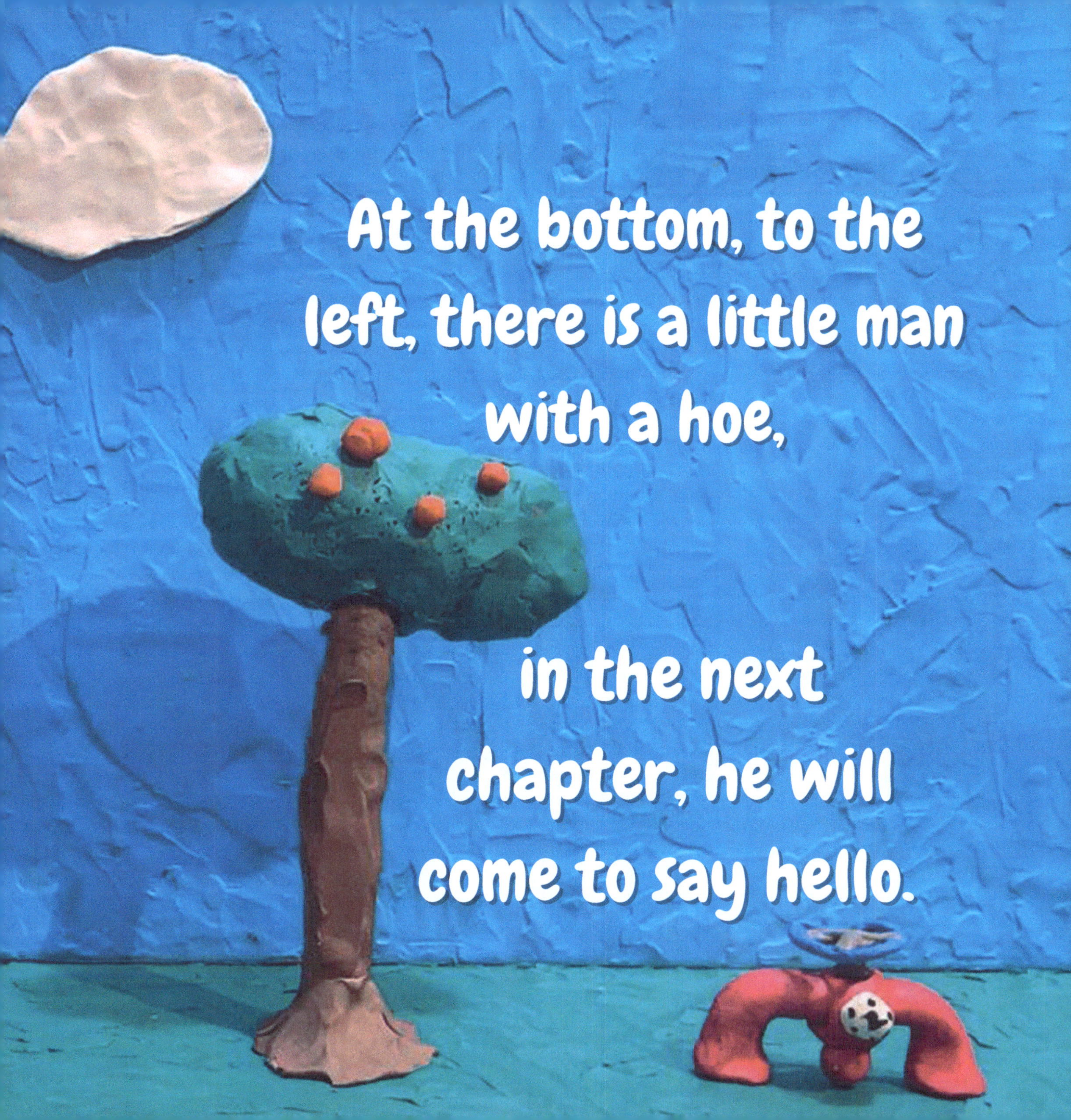
At the bottom, to the
left, there is a little man
with a hoe,

in the next
chapter, he will
come to say hello.

THE END.

The orchard

The story of the orchard begins in 1886 when my grandfather's grandfather, Yechiel Trachtenberg, immigrated to Israel from Bessarabia.

He was a farmer and the head of the city of Rishon LeZion's council.

Over the years, the agricultural lands were handed down from generation to generation until they reached my mother, Talya Tal. Her husband takes care of these lands today, and his name is

Raphael, the farmer, my dad.

Did you like it?
GIVE US A REVIEW /BUY SOMEONE A GIFT

www.ingramcontent.com/pod-product-compliance
Lightning Source LLC
LaVergne TN
LVHW071624180726
843512LV00002B/239